COMMUNITY CONNECTIONS

WHAT SHOULD I DO?

WHAT SHOULD I DO?
NEAR A BUSY STREET

BY WIL MARA

CHERRY
LAKE
Publishing

Published in the United States of America by Cherry Lake Publishing
Ann Arbor, Michigan
www.cherrylakepublishing.com

Content Adviser: Karen Sheehan, MD, MPH, Children's Memorial Hospital, Chicago, Illinois

Photo Credits: Cover and page 17 ©Blend Images/Alamy; page 5,
©Sergei Poromov/Dreamstime.com; page 7, ©George Fairbairn/Shutterstock, Inc.; page 9,
©Andrey Shadrin/Shutterstock, Inc.; page 11, ©Patti McConville/Alamy; page 13,
©Feng Yu/Shutterstock, Inc.; page 15, ©Susan Leggett/Dreamstime.com; page 19,
©Maggie Robinson/Alamy; page 21, ©Heather Renee/Shutterstock, Inc.

LIBRARY OF CONGRESS CATALOGING-IN-PUBLICATION DATA
Mara, Wil.
  What should I do? Near a busy street/by Wil Mara.
     p. cm.—(Community connections)
  Includes bibliographical references and index.
  ISBN-13: 978-1-61080-051-8 (lib. bdg.)
  ISBN-10: 1-61080-051-6 (lib. bdg.)
  1. Safety education—Juvenile literature. 2. Streets—Juvenile literature.
  3. Traffic safety and children—Juvenile literature. 4. City
and town life—Juvenile literature. I. Title.
  HV675.M26 2011
  613.6—dc22   2010052615

Cherry Lake Publishing would like to acknowledge the
work of The Partnership for 21st Century Skills. Please
visit www.21stcenturyskills.org for more information.

Printed in the United States of America
Corporate Graphics Inc.
July 2011
CLFA09

NEAR A BUSY STREET

CONTENTS

4 A Dangerous Place

6 Not Everyone Drives Safely

10 Some Simple Rules

20 Other Important Safety Rules

22 Glossary

23 Find Out More

24 Index

24 About the Author

WHAT SHOULD I DO?

A DANGEROUS PLACE

Busy streets can be very **dangerous**. **Traffic** moves fast. You could get hurt if you are not careful. You should always follow safety rules when you are near a street.

Cars might be moving at speeds of more than 40 miles (64 kilometers) per hour on busy streets.

Look at the busy streets near your home. Do you notice any dangers? How might someone walking near the street get hurt? What can people do to avoid getting hurt?

NOT EVERYONE DRIVES SAFELY

You might think drivers are watching out for you. But not all of them are. Sometimes they get **distracted**. Maybe their cell phones ring. Maybe they are looking for street signs. They might not see you at all.

Drivers who use cell phones while driving cause more than 1 million accidents each year.

It is always a good idea to watch the people who are driving. You might notice that their eyes are not on the road or on you. Just because you can see a car doesn't mean the driver can see you!

7

Drivers sometimes lose control of their cars because a road is wet or icy. Drivers can also lose control if one of their tires blows out.

Remember that cars and trucks are made of metal. They are very heavy. It would hurt very much to get hit by a car. You could even die.

Some car tires don't grip the road well when streets are wet.

SOME SIMPLE RULES

You can help keep yourself safe by following a few simple rules. First, stay as far away from the street as you can. Stay away from the **curb** when you are walking on a sidewalk.

People who live in big cities must be extra careful when crossing very busy streets.

11

Always use a **crosswalk** to cross the street. Do not cross until every car stops moving. Get to the other side of the street as quickly as you can. But don't run! Never cross from between two parked cars. Drivers will not be able to see you.

A clearly marked crosswalk helps keep everyone safe.

13

Sometimes you might ride your bicycle near a road. Always wear your helmet and other **safety gear**.

Do not ride in the street unless you have to. Always ride on the right-hand side of the road. Get off your bicycle and walk with it when you need to cross the street.

Riding your bicycle on the sidewalk can help keep you safe from passing cars.

Be extra careful at corners. You can never tell what might be around a corner. There might be a driveway on the other side. A car coming out of the driveway will not be able to see you. You will not see the car, either. Stop at corners and look around to make sure no cars are coming.

Always be careful near driveways. A driver who is backing out might not see you.

Why do you think corners are so dangerous? You can get hurt even if a car is moving very slowly. Can you guess why?

17

Streets can be even more dangerous at night. Never walk or ride your bicycle near a street that does not have lights.

Always wear brightly colored clothes. You should also wear **reflective tape**. This will make it easier for drivers to see you.

Brightly colored clothes will help drivers see you in the daytime, too.

OTHER IMPORTANT SAFETY RULES

You must always pay attention near busy streets. Never wear headphones. You will not be able to hear any cars coming. Do not chase toys, people, or animals into the street.

Streets can be dangerous. But you will stay safe if you pay attention and follow the rules!

Make sure you know the safest way to get to school and other places you walk to often.

Make a map of your town. Mark the places you go most often. Then draw lines showing how to get to those places without going near busy roads. Those are the ways you should always go.

21

GLOSSARY

crosswalk (KROSS-wok) marked lines that show the right place to cross a street

curb (KURB) the raised edge of the sidewalk where it meets the road

dangerous (DAYN-jur-us) potentially harmful

distracted (dis-TRAK-tid) unable to pay attention

reflective tape (re-FLEK-tiv TAYP) a type of tape that shines when light hits it

safety gear (SAYF-tee GEER) pads and helmets that people wear to protect their bodies

traffic (TRAF-ik) all of the vehicles on a road

FIND OUT MORE

BOOKS

Barraclough, Sue. *Road Safety*. Chicago: Heinemann Library, 2008.

Llewellyn, Claire. *Watch Out! On the Road*. Hauppauge, NY: Barron's Educational Series, 2006.

Mattern, Joanne. *Staying Safe on My Bike*. Milwaukee: Weekly Reader Early Learning Library, 2007.

WEB SITES

KidsHealth—Bike Safety
kidshealth.org/kid/watch/out/bike_safety.html
Read more about staying safe when you ride your bike.

Safe Walking for Kids
www.safeny.ny.gov/Kids/kidswalk.html
Learn about the signs and traffic lights that can help keep you safe.

INDEX

bicycles, 14, 18
blow-outs, 8

cars, 4, 7, 8, 12,
    16, 17, 20
clothes, 18
corners, 16, 17
crosswalks, 12, 14
curbs, 10

danger, 4, 5, 17,
    18, 20
distractions, 6, 7
drivers, 6, 7, 8, 12,
    18
driveways, 16

headphones, 20

maps, 21

reflective tape,
    18
rules, 4, 10, 12,
    14, 16, 18, 20

sidewalks, 10
street lights, 18
street signs, 6

tires, 8
traffic, 4

ABOUT THE AUTHOR

Wil Mara is the award-winning author of more than 120 books, many of which are educational titles for children. More information about his work can be found at *www.wilmara.com.*